D0348477

Cool
CAKES & CUPCAKES

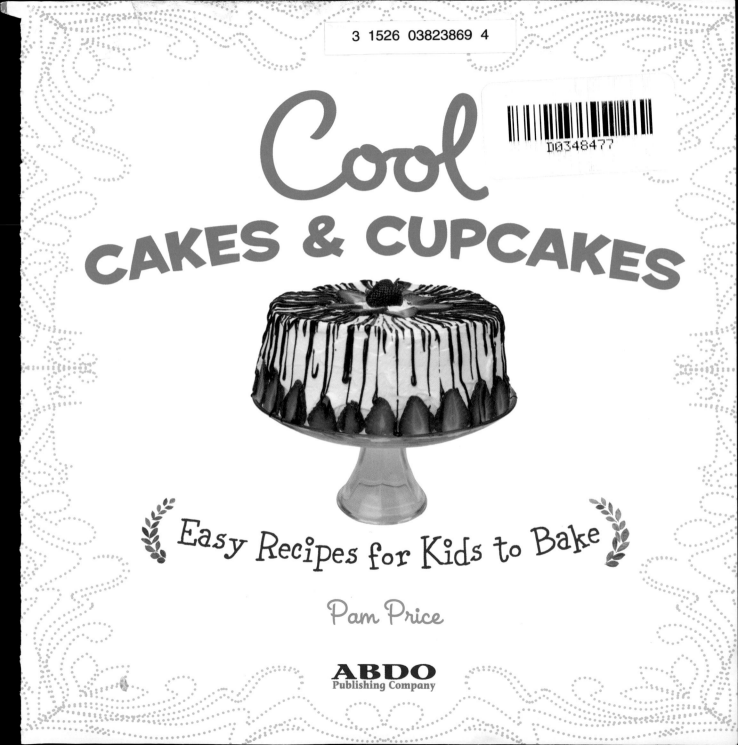

Easy Recipes for Kids to Bake

Pam Price

ABDO
Publishing Company

TO ADULT HELPERS

You're invited to assist up-and-coming pastry chefs in a kitchen near you! And it will pay off in many ways. Your children will develop new skills, gain confidence, and make some delicious treats while learning to bake. What's more, it's going to be a lot of fun.

These recipes are designed to let children bake independently as much as possible. Encourage them to do whatever they are able to do on their own. Also encourage them to try any variations supplied with the recipes and to experiment with their own ideas. Building creativity into the baking process encourages children to think like real chefs.

Before getting started, set some ground rules about using the kitchen, cooking tools, and ingredients. Most important, adult supervision is a must whenever a child uses the oven, stove, or sharp tools.

So put on your aprons and stand by. Let your young bakers take the lead. Watch and learn. Taste their creations. Praise their efforts. Enjoy the culinary adventure!

Editor: Liz Salzmann
Series Concept: Nancy Tuminelly
Cover and Interior Design: Anders Hanson, Mighty Media, Inc.
Photo Credits: Anders Hanson, Shutterstock

The following manufacturers/names appearing in this book are trademarks: Arm & Hammer®, C&H®, Kraft® Calumet®, Land O' Lakes®, Lunds® and Byerly's®, McCormick®, Morton®, Proctor Silex®, Pyrex®, Roundy's®

Library of Congress Cataloging-in-Publication Data

Price, Pamela S.
  Cool cakes & cupcakes : easy recipes for kids to bake / Pam Price.
     p. cm. -- (Cool baking)
  Includes bibliographical references and index.
  ISBN 978-1-60453-774-1 (alk. paper)
  1. Cake--Juvenile literature. 2. Cupcakes--Juvenile literature. 3. Baking--Juvenile literature. I. Title.
  TX771.P698 2010
  641.8'653--dc22
                    2009027373

Table of Contents

Baking Is Cool

When it comes to baking, the possibilities are endless!

Cake is a **versatile** dessert. We make fancy cakes for celebrations such as birthdays and weddings. We make simple, homey cakes to welcome new neighbors. Cakes can have one layer or many. You can top them with icing, whipped cream, powdered sugar, or nothing at all.

So, as you might imagine, cakes can be very hard to make. And, they can be very simple to make! In this book, you'll find recipes for cakes that may seem complicated, but they are actually fairly simple to prepare. So tie on an apron, grab a whisk, and get busy in the kitchen!

GET THE PICTURE!

When a step number in a recipe has a colored circle around it, look for the picture that goes with it. The circle around the photo will be the same color as the step number.

Ready, Set, Bake!

Preparation is a key element of successful baking.
Here are some things to keep in mind.

ASK PERMISSION

> Get permission to use the kitchen, baking tools, and ingredients.

> If you'd like to do something by yourself, say so. As long as you can do it safely, do it!

> Ask for help when you need it. Professional chefs have *sous chefs*, which means "assistant chefs" in French. You can have one too!

BE PREPARED

Read the whole recipe the day before you plan to bake.

> Make sure you have all the ingredients. Do you need to go to the grocery store?

> Will there be enough time? For example, cakes need to cool completely before you frost them.

When it's time to bake, these steps will help you be organized.

> Gather all the tools and equipment you will need.

> Prepare the pans as directed and preheat the oven.

> Gather the listed ingredients. Sometimes you need prepared ingredients such as chopped nuts or sifted flour. Do those prep jobs as you gather the ingredients.

> Finally, do the recipe steps in the order they are listed.

Safety First!

When you bake you need to use an oven. Sometimes you also have to use sharp tools. Ask an adult helper to be in the kitchen with you. Here's how to keep it safe.

HOT STUFF

> Set up a cooling rack ahead of time.

> Make sure it's easy to get from the oven to the cooling area. There should be no people or things in the way.

> Always use oven mitts, not towels, when handling hot pots and pans.

> The oven is hot too. Don't bump into the racks or the door.

THAT'S SHARP

> Choose a small knife. Cut just a small amount of food at a time.

> Always keep your other hand away from the blade.

> Work slowly and keep your eyes on the knife.

SUPER SHARP!

In this book, you will see this symbol beside some recipes. It means you need to use a knife for those recipes. Ask an adult to stand by.

Germ Alert!

It's so tempting, but you shouldn't eat batter that contains raw eggs. Raw eggs may contain salmonella **bacteria**, which can cause food poisoning. Eating batter that contains raw eggs might make you sick. Really sick! Ask an adult if it's okay to lick bowls, beaters, and spoons.

KEEP IT CLEAN

> Tie back long hair.

> Wash your hands before you begin baking. Rub them with soap for 20 seconds before rinsing. Wash them again if you eat, sneeze, cough, take a bathroom break, or touch the trash container.

> Use clean tools and equipment. If you lick a spoon, wash it before using it again.

> Make sure that your cutting board hasn't had raw meat on it.

Tools of the Trade

These are the basic tools used for baking cakes. Each recipe in this book lists the tools you will need.

8-INCH ROUND CAKE PAN

9 × 5-INCH LOAF PAN

MUFFIN TIN

TUBE PAN

BUNDT PAN

DOUBLE BOILER

SCISSORS

PENCIL

WAXED PAPER

CUPCAKE PAPERS

MEASURING CUPS

MEASURING SPOONS

MIXER AND BEATERS

MIXING BOWLS

WHISK

SILICONE SPATULA

WOODEN SPOON

SPOON

SMALL SCOOP

SIFTER

WOODEN SKEWERS OR TOOTHPICKS

COOLING RACK

OVEN MITTS

SERVING PLATTER

SMALL KNIFE AND CUTTING BOARD

BUTTER KNIFE

FROSTING SPATULA

SERRATED KNIFE

ZESTER

Cool Ingredients

Butter, flour, sugar. You can make many different goodies based on these three ingredients! Add a few others, and the possibilities are endless.

BUTTER

Choose unsalted butter for baking. You add salt in most recipes. Using unsalted butter keeps the dough from having too much salt.

FLOUR

In a recipe, the word *flour* means all-purpose wheat flour. But other grains can be ground into flour too. Some of these grains include kamut, rye, buckwheat, and corn.

SUGAR

You use several types of sugar for baking. Most common are granulated sugar, powdered sugar, and brown sugar. Sometimes a recipe may call for corn syrup, molasses, or honey. If a recipe just says *sugar*, it means granulated sugar.

About Organics

Organic foods are grown without **synthetic** fertilizers and **pesticides**. This is good for the earth. And, recent studies show that organic foods may be more nutritious than **conventionally** grown foods.

Organic foods used to be hard to find. But now you can find organic versions of most foods. Organic foods are more expensive than conventionally grown foods. Families must decide for themselves whether to spend extra for organic foods.

SALT

You may be surprised to see salt in a dessert recipe. Salt is a flavor **enhancer**. It enhances the flavors in your baked goods, whether they are sweet or **savory**.

EXTRACTS

There are many flavoring **extracts** used in baking. Some of these are vanilla, lemon, and maple. You will probably use vanilla extract most often. Vanilla extract is made from the beans, or seedpods, of tropical orchids.

EGGS

Eggs come in many sizes. Use large eggs unless the recipe says otherwise. Bring eggs to room temperature before you add them to the batter.

BAKING SODA AND BAKING POWDER

Baking soda and baking powder are common **leavening** agents. Leavening agents are ingredients that make baked goods rise.

FRUIT

Sometimes recipes call for citrus zest. The zest is the colored part of the citrus fruit's skin. The oils in the skins are very flavorful, so a little zest goes a long way!

CHOCOLATE

Chocolate comes from the bean of the cacao tree. When cocoa beans are processed, the cocoa particles and the cocoa butter are separated. Then they are recombined in different **formulas** such as semisweet, bittersweet, and milk chocolate. In general, the higher the cocoa content, the stronger the taste. In a recipe, *cocoa* refers to a powder made from ground cocoa beans. It is not the same thing as powdered hot chocolate mix!

MILK AND CREAM

You can use whatever milk you have, whether it is skim, low fat, or whole milk. Substituting usually won't noticeably affect the quality of what you're making. However, use cream or buttermilk if a recipe says to. You can make buttermilk if you don't have any. Put one tablespoon of white vinegar in a measuring cup. Then add milk until you have one cup of liquid.

NUTS

Nuts, usually walnuts or pecans, add flavor to baked goods. Luckily, you can buy them already sliced or chopped!

Allergy Alert

Millions of people have food allergies or food intolerance. Foods that most often cause allergic reactions include milk, eggs, peanuts, tree nuts, and wheat. Common food intolerances include lactose and gluten. Lactose is the sugar in milk. Gluten is the protein in wheat.

Baked goods can be a real hazard for people with food allergies or intolerances. If a friend cannot eat the goodies you're offering, don't be offended. It could be a life or death matter for your friend.

Cool Techniques

These are the techniques that bakers use. If you can't remember how to do something, just reread these pages.

MEASURING DRY INGREDIENTS

Dip the measuring spoon or measuring cup into whatever you're measuring. Use a butter knife to scrape off the excess.

MIXING DRY INGREDIENTS

Unless the recipe says otherwise, always stir the dry ingredients together first. Measure them into a bowl and stir them with a fork or a whisk.

CREAMING

Creaming means beating something until it is smooth and creamy. When baking, you often need to cream butter. Unless the recipe says otherwise, use butter that is near room temperature.

WHIPPING CREAM

Pour the whipping cream into a chilled bowl with deep sides. Beat on high speed until the cream forms peaks. Don't overbeat, or you will make butter!

SCRAPING A BOWL

When using a mixer, turn off the mixer occasionally. Then scrape the sides and bottom of the bowl with a silicone spatula. That way you'll be sure that all of the ingredients are completely mixed. Recipes don't usually mention this important step. You just have to remember to do it!

ZESTING CITRUS FRUIT

Gently scrape the fruit over the small holes of a grater or a citrus zester. Just remove the colored part of the skin. Then chop the zest with a small knife. The pieces should be no longer than ¼ inch.

GREASING A PAN

Butter wrappers are great for greasing pans. If you don't have one, use waxed paper and a bit of butter. Rub the butter all around the inside of the pan. There should be a light coating of butter on the bottom and sides.

FLOURING A PAN

Sometimes you will need to flour the pan after you grease it. Sprinkle about a tablespoon of flour in the greased pan. Hold the pan over the sink with one hand. Tap its side firmly with the other hand. As you tap, twist and turn the pan to move the flour around. When all the surfaces are lightly coated, dump out the extra flour.

MELTING CHOCOLATE

To melt chocolate on the stove, use a double boiler. Put a little water in the bottom part. Put the chocolate in the top part. Turn the burner on low. Simmer the water until the chocolate melts. Stir often.

To melt chocolate in a microwave, use medium power. After 30 seconds, stir the chocolate. Then heat it again for another 30 seconds. You may have to do this several times before all the chocolate melts.

Word Order Counts!

Pay attention to word order in the ingredients list. If it says "1 cup sifted flour," that means you sift some flour and then measure it. If the list says "1 cup flour, sifted," that means you measure first and then sift. Believe it or not, this makes a difference. Sifted flour is fluffier than unsifted flour. This means less of it fits in the measuring cup.

TESTING A CAKE FOR DONENESS

There are three ways to check whether a cake is done. First, remove the cake from the oven. Then use one or more of these methods to decide if it is done. If the cake isn't done, put it back in the oven. Check it again in a few minutes.

1. Gently tap the middle of the cake. It will spring back up if it is done.

2. Examine the edges of the cake. They will pull away from the sides of the pan when the cake is done.

3. Stick a tester into the center of the cake and pull it back out. You can use a sharp knife, a wooden skewer, or a toothpick. If no gooey batter sticks to the tester, the cake is done.

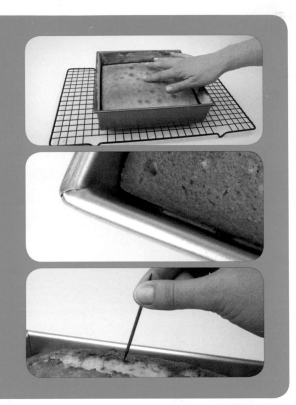

REMOVING A CAKE FROM A PAN

Put the cake pan on a cooling rack for about 5 minutes. Insert a butter knife between the cake and the side of the pan. Run it all the way around the cake once.

Put the cooling rack upside down on the top of the cake pan. Carefully hold the rack against the cake pan and turn them over together. Now the cake pan is upside down on top of the rack. Lightly tap the cake pan. Then lift it off of the cake. Always let a cake cool completely before frosting it.

Cat in the Hat Cupcakes

MAKES
24 CUPCAKES

Make these cupcakes for a party or for Valentine's Day!

INGREDIENTS

FOR THE CUPCAKES

2¼ cups cake flour

2 tablespoons unsweetened cocoa powder, plus extra for preparing the pans

2 teaspoons cinnamon

1¼ teaspoons baking powder

¼ teaspoon baking soda

¾ teaspoon salt

¾ cup (1½ sticks) butter at room temperature

1½ cups sugar

2 eggs at room temperature, slightly beaten

1 ounce liquid red food coloring

2 teaspoons vanilla extract

1 teaspoon cider vinegar

1 cup buttermilk

FOR THE FROSTING

¾ cup (1½ sticks) of butter at room temperature

6 cups of powdered sugar, sifted

about ½ cup whole or 2% milk

1 tablespoon vanilla extract

TOOLS: sifter, muffin tin, mixing bowls, measuring cups, measuring spoons, whisk, mixer and beaters, silicone spatula, wooden skewer, cooling rack, oven mitts, serrated knife, frosting spatula

TO MAKE THE CUPCAKES

 1 Grease all of the cups in a muffin tin. "Flour" the cups with cocoa powder. Preheat the oven to 350 degrees.

2 Place the flour, 2 tablespoons of cocoa powder, cinnamon, baking powder, baking soda, and salt in a mixing bowl. Blend the dry ingredients well with a whisk.

 3 In another mixing bowl, cream the butter. Then beat in the sugar until it is light and fluffy. This will take about 5 minutes. Be sure to stop the mixer and scrape the sides of the bowl often. Add the eggs and beat until the eggs are well mixed in.

4 Add the food coloring, vanilla, and vinegar and blend well. The batter should be a solid red color with no streaks.

5 Add about a third of the flour mixture and the buttermilk. Beat on low speed just until blended. Add half of the remaining flour mixture and half of the remaining buttermilk. Beat on low just until blended. Repeat with the remaining flour mixture and buttermilk.

6 Use a small measuring cup to put batter into each cup in the tin. Fill the cups about three-fourths full.

7 Bake for about 25 minutes or until a wood skewer inserted into a cupcake comes out clean. Cool on a cooling rack for about 5 minutes. Then remove the cupcakes from the tin. Leave the cupcakes on the rack until they cool completely.

TO MAKE THE FROSTING

1   Cream the butter until it is light and fluffy.

2   Add one-fourth of the powdered sugar and one-fourth of the milk. Starting with the mixer on low speed, beat until smooth.

3   Continue beating in small amounts of the milk and the powdered sugar. Each time you add more, start with the mixer on low. Then increase the mixer speed. Otherwise you'll create a cloud of powdered sugar.

4   Stop beating when the frosting is thick enough to spread. Note that you may not need to add all of the milk. Finally, beat in the vanilla.

5   Use a serrated knife to cut each cupcake in half across the middle. Spread a thick layer of frosting on each bottom half.

6   Put each cupcake top on a frosted bottom. Then frost the top of each cupcake.

Luscious Lemon Pound Cake

The original pound cake recipe called for a pound each of butter, sugar, flour, and eggs!

MAKES 8 TO 10 SERVINGS

INGREDIENTS

- 2 cups flour
- ½ teaspoon salt
- ½ teaspoon baking powder
- 1 cup butter
- 1½ cups sugar
- 3 eggs
- 1 teaspoon lemon extract
- zest of one lemon, finely grated or chopped
- 1 cup of milk at room temperature
- ice cream & fresh berries (optional)

TOOLS: 9 × 5-inch loaf pan   measuring cups   mixing bowls   mixer and beaters   wooden skewer   cooling rack
zester   measuring spoons   whisk   silicone spatula   oven mitts

1 Grease and flour the loaf pan and set it aside. Preheat the oven to 350 degrees.

2 Whisk together the flour, salt, and baking powder. Set this bowl aside.

3 Put the butter and sugar in another mixing bowl. Beat until light and fluffy.

4 Add the eggs one at a time. Beat for about a minute after adding each egg. Then beat in the lemon **extract** and the lemon zest.

5 Add about a third of the flour mixture and about a third of the milk. Beat on low speed just until mixed.

6 Add half of the remaining flour mixture and half of the remaining milk. Beat on low speed just until mixed. Then add the remaining flour mixture and milk. Beat on low just until mixed.

7 Pour the batter into the prepared loaf pan. Bake for about 60 to 75 minutes. Insert a wooden skewer to check for doneness. Crumbs will stick to the skewer when the cake is done.

8 Place the pan on the cooling rack for about 30 minutes. Then remove the cake from the pan and let it cool completely on the rack.

9 To serve, cut the cake into slices about an inch thick. Serve the cake plain or with ice cream and fresh berries.

Heavenly Angel Food Cake

Nine out of ten angels love it!

MAKES 10 SERVINGS

INGREDIENTS

- 1 angel food cake mix, plus ingredients listed on its box
- 1 pint heavy whipping cream
- 2 tablespoons powdered sugar, sifted
- 1 teaspoon vanilla extract
- 2 cups strawberries, blueberries, or raspberries, rinsed and drained
- chocolate sauce (optional)

TOOLS:

sifter
measuring cups

measuring spoons
mixing bowl

mixer and beaters
silicone spatula

tube pan
oven mitts

serving platter
knife

1 Make the cake following the directions on the package.

2 Remove the cake from the oven. Set the pan upside down on its feet or hang it on the neck of a glass bottle. Let the cake cool completely before removing it from the pan. Place the cake on a large, round platter.

3 Wait until you are just about ready to serve the cake. Then whip the cream until it starts thickening. Sprinkle on the powdered sugar and pour in the vanilla. Then continue beating on high speed until the cream is fluffy. Remember not to overbeat the cream!

4 Use a silicone spatula to spread the whipped cream all over the cake.

5 Arrange the berries on top of the cake and around the bottom edge. If you like, **drizzle** chocolate sauce over the top of the cake.

Tip

Here's how to avoid flattening an angel food cake when you cut it. Use a serrated knife and hold it straight up and down. Using a gentle sawing motion, cut from the center out to the edge of the cake.

Tunnel of Fudge Cake

When you cut into the cake, you'll see where it gets its name!

INGREDIENTS

FOR THE CAKE

2¼ cups flour

¾ cup unsweetened cocoa powder, plus extra for preparing the pan

2 cups chopped walnuts

1¾ cups (3½ sticks) butter

1¾ cups sugar

6 eggs

2 cups powdered sugar

FOR THE GLAZE

¾ cup powdered sugar

¼ cup unsweetened cocoa powder

¼ to ⅜ cup milk

TOOLS: Bundt pan · small knife · cutting board · measuring cups · mixing bowls · whisk · mixer and beaters · silicone spatula · wooden spoon · cooling rack · oven mitts · serving platter · spoon

1. Grease the pan and "flour" it with cocoa powder. Make sure you get all the nooks and crannies. The cake will stick to any part that isn't coated. Preheat the oven to 350 degrees.

2. Put the flour and the cocoa powder in a mixing bowl. Stir with a whisk to combine them. Stir in the chopped walnuts. Set the bowl aside.

3. Cream the butter. Then beat in the sugar until the mixture is light and fluffy. Add the eggs one at a time. Beat well after you add each one.

4. With the mixer on low speed, gradually pour in the powdered sugar. Continue beating until the mixture is well blended.

5. Pour the flour and nut mixture into the batter. Stir with a wooden spoon until all of the flour is mixed in.

6. Pour the batter into the prepared pan. Smooth the top of the batter with a silicone spatula.

7. Bake for 45 minutes or until the cake pulls away from the sides of the pan. Set the pan on the cooling rack. Let the cake cool in the pan for 90 minutes.

8. Place a serving platter upside down over the top of the cake pan. Carefully turn the platter and the pan over together. Gently remove the cake pan. Let the cake cool completely for another 2 hours.

9. Make the glaze in a small mixing bowl. Whisk together the powdered sugar, cocoa powder, and half of the milk. If the glaze is too thick to **drizzle**, add a little more milk.

10. Use a spoon to drizzle the glaze over the cake.

Chocolate Flourless Cake

Because there is no flour in this cake, it's like a dense, moist brownie!

MAKES 8 TO 10 SERVINGS

INGREDIENTS

- 4 ounces bittersweet (not unsweetened) chocolate chips
- ½ cup butter
- ¾ cup sugar
- 3 large eggs
- 1 teaspoon vanilla extract
- ½ cup unsweetened cocoa powder
- powdered sugar
- chocolate sauce (optional)
- raspberries (optional)

TOOLS:

8-inch round cake pan	pencil	measuring spoons	silicone spatula	sifter	butter knife
	scissors	double boiler	mixing bowl	oven mitts	serving platter
waxed paper	measuring cups	wooden spoon	whisk	cooling rack	

1 Trace the bottom of the cake pan on waxed paper. Cut out the circle. Grease the cake pan. Place the circle of waxed paper in the bottom of the pan. Grease the waxed paper. Preheat the oven to 375 degrees.

2 Set up the double boiler. Put the chocolate and the butter in the top pan. Melt the chocolate and butter over low heat. Stir occasionally as the chocolate and butter melt. Remove the melted chocolate mixture from the heat.

3 In a mixing bowl, whisk together the sugar, eggs, and vanilla. Pour in the chocolate mixture and whisk until blended.

4 Sift the cocoa powder into the mixture and whisk just until combined.

5 Pour the cake batter into the prepared pan. Bake for 25 minutes. Leave the cake in the pan. Place it on a cooling rack for 5 minutes.

6 Run a butter knife around the edge of the pan. Next, place the serving platter upside down on the cake pan. Carefully turn the platter and cake pan over together. The pan will be on top of the plate. Remove the cake pan and gently peel away the waxed paper.

7 Put some powdered sugar in a sifter or a small sieve. Tap the side gently while moving it around over the cake. If you like, **drizzle** some chocolate sauce over the top. Try serving it with fresh raspberries!

Secret Center Cupcakes

MAKES 12 CUPCAKES

What's hiding in the center of these cupcakes? Only the chef knows!

INGREDIENTS

FOR THE CUPCAKES

1½ cups flour

½ teaspoon salt

1 teaspoon baking soda

¼ cup unsweetened cocoa powder

⅓ cup vegetable oil

1 cup water

1 cup sugar

1 tablespoon white vinegar

1 teaspoon vanilla extract

FOR THE FILLING

8 ounces cream cheese at room temperature

1 egg

½ teaspoon salt

⅓ cup sugar

1 cup chocolate chips

FOR THE TOPPING

2 teaspoons cinnamon

2 teaspoons sugar

¼ cup sliced almonds

TOOLS: muffin tin, cupcake papers, mixing bowls, measuring cups, measuring spoons, whisk, wooden spoon, mixer and beaters, silicone spatula, spoon or small scoop, cooling rack, oven mitts

1 Place a cupcake paper in each cup of the muffin tin. Preheat the oven to 350 degrees.

2 In a mixing bowl, whisk together the flour, salt, baking soda, and cocoa powder. Set the bowl aside.

3 In another mixing bowl, whisk together the vegetable oil, water, sugar, vinegar, and vanilla. Stir in the dry ingredients. Mix with a wooden spoon until the batter is smooth.

4 For the filling, put the cream cheese, egg, salt, and sugar in a small mixing bowl. Beat just until smooth. Stir in the chocolate chips.

5 Fill each cup half full with the chocolate batter. Then drop a small spoonful of the cream cheese filling on top of the batter. The batter will rise around the filling when you bake the cupcakes.

6 For the topping, stir together the cinnamon and sugar. Place a few almond slices on top of each cupcake. Then sprinkle a little of the cinnamon-sugar over the almonds.

7 Bake for about 35 minutes. Cool the cupcakes on a rack for about 10 minutes. Then remove them from the pan. Leave the cupcakes on the rack until they are completely cool.

Wrap It Up!

Tips for keeping the treats you make fresh and delicious!

Most cakes don't keep for very long. So, always tightly cover any leftover cake with plastic wrap. Store the leftover cake in the refrigerator.

Cakes make great gifts for special occasions. You can make a cake to celebrate a birthday or the first day of summer break. And your new neighbors will surely appreciate some homemade cupcakes.

Here's a trick for when you're taking a cake somewhere. Make a disposable cake plate! Then you don't have to worry about getting your plate back. Just cut a piece of cardboard that is a little bigger than the cake. Then cover the cardboard with aluminum foil. Now you have a fancy plate that you don't have to worry about!